3/15

Derrick Rose

By Jon M. Fishman

AMAZING ATHLETES

Lerner Publications Company • Minneapolis

Lerner Publications Company
A division of Lerner Publishing Group, Inc.
241 First Avenue North
Minneapolis, MN 55401 USA

For reading levels and more information, look up this title at www.lernerbooks.com.

Library of Congress Cataloging-in-Publication Data

Fishman, Jon M.
    Derrick Rose / by Jon M. Fishman.
       pages   cm. — (Amazing athletes)
    Includes index.
    ISBN 978–1–4677–3677–0 (lib. bdg. : alk. paper)
    ISBN 978–1–4677–4586–4 (eBook)
    1. Rose, Derrick—Juvenile literature. 2. Basketball players—United States—Biography—
Juvenile literature. I. Title.
    GV884.R619F57 2015
    796.323092—dc23 [B]   2013050214

Manufactured in the United States of America
1 – BP – 7/15/14

TABLE OF CONTENTS

Derrick Rose plays for the Chicago Bulls.

A HEROIC RETURN

On November 31, 2013, Derrick Rose stepped onto the basketball court during a game for the first time in more than a year. The Chicago Bulls **point guard** had missed the entire 2012–2013 season with a knee injury. He was finally healthy enough to play again.

The Bulls fans at United Center in Chicago were happy to see Derrick back in action. Derrick is one of the most explosive players in the National Basketball Association (NBA). Fans are stunned by his ability to zip around the court and soar for huge **slam dunks**. But Derrick isn't just a flashy player. He's also one of the most skilled. He was named NBA Most Valuable Player (MVP) for the 2010–2011 season.

Derrick (*center*) squeaks past the New York Knicks' defense.

It's not easy to stop Derrick when he's heading for the basket.

Derrick and the Bulls were playing against the New York Knicks on November 31. The crowd chanted "MVP! MVP!" when Chicago's young point guard took the floor. He seemed like his old self. He made **layups** and **three-point shots**. He grabbed **rebounds** and made **assists** with pinpoint passes.

The game was close from beginning to end. New York had the lead, 81–80, with about 10 seconds left in the game. Chicago had the ball. Everyone in the arena knew that Derrick would take the next shot for his team. The best players step up when the game is on the line.

Derrick dribbled the ball to the **baseline**. Two New York defenders moved with him. Derrick rose up and lofted a shot over both defenders. The ball floated in a high arc before falling through the basket. Chicago had the lead, 82–81!

Derrick jumps up to sink the winning shot for the Bulls.

When New York's Carmelo Anthony missed a shot a few seconds later, the game was over. The Bulls had won!

Fans believe Derrick could lead the Bulls to an NBA championship.

It was a big win for Chicago. Even better, Derrick was healthy and leading his team again. He'd never had any doubts that he'd be back. "I work too hard," he said after the game. "Just going to continue to keep building and keep getting better."

The Bulls won the NBA championship six times in the 1990s. Those teams were led by megastar Michael Jordan.

With support from his mother and brothers, Derrick (*second from right*) overcame the challenges of growing up in a tough neighborhood.

BROTHERLY LOVE

Chicago, Illinois, is a basketball city. The Bulls are one of the most successful teams in NBA history. NBA stars such as Dwyane Wade grew up there. And high school and college basketball is a big deal. Derrick Martell Rose was born in this basketball-loving city on October 4, 1988.

Dwyane Wade (*right*) played for the Harold L. Richards High School in a Chicago suburb before he went on to NBA stardom.

Derrick grew up with his mother, Brenda, and three older brothers—Dwayne, Reggie, and Allan. His father was not part of the family.

Chicago's Englewood neighborhood, where the Rose family lived, has many problems. Most people in the neighborhood are poor. Drug dealing and violence are common. But Brenda raised her four sons to avoid these concerns. "My mom would walk down the street and drag us home if she heard we were getting into trouble," Dwayne said.

All the Rose boys loved to play basketball. By the time Derrick was in seventh grade, it was clear that he had a special talent for the game.

Englewood, a neighborhood on Chicago's South Side, is known for frequent crime and few job opportunities. Families like Derrick's struggle to get by.

Children and adults enjoy a newly rebuilt basketball court in Englewood. Many people hope the court will help keep kids off the dangerous streets.

Word began to spread through the city about the young player. Robert Smith, a basketball coach at Chicago's Simeon Career Academy, watched Derrick play in 2002. Smith liked what he saw. "He was doing things that a normal seventh grader couldn't do and that some juniors and seniors in high school couldn't do," the coach said.

As word got around about Derrick's ability, more and more people tried to get in touch with the young player. Some had good intentions. Others didn't. "People were just beginning to really look at how they could make money off Derrick," said Reggie.

Brenda was concerned. She knew Derrick was too young to judge who wanted to help him and who wanted to take advantage of him. But Derrick's older brothers knew the Chicago basketball scene. Brenda asked Reggie, Dwayne, and Allan to protect Derrick. "His brothers knew basketball. I didn't," Brenda said. "I told them to handle it."

At Simeon Career Academy, Derrick became a high school basketball legend.

IN HIS OWN TIME

In 2003, Derrick enrolled at Simeon Career Academy as a freshman. The Rose family chose the high school because of its reputation for safety. Derrick also liked coach Robert Smith.

Many people at Simeon thought Derrick was good enough to play on the **varsity** team his first year. But he opted to stay with his freshman team. "We didn't want to single him out from the other freshmen," Reggie said.

Derrick wanted to fit in with his teammates. But his unique talent was obvious whenever he stepped onto the court. The pressure to move up to the next level grew even more intense after Derrick led his freshman team to the 2004 city championship.

The varsity team was about to compete in the state tournament.

For Derrick (*right*), being a team player was more important than getting extra attention.

At Simeon, Derrick wore the No. 25 jersey. The school retired the number in 2009.

Coach Smith wanted Derrick to join the team. But once again, Derrick turned down the opportunity to move up. "He didn't want to overshadow the kids that worked hard to get us downstate," Coach Smith said.

Derrick waited to join varsity until the 2004–2005 basketball season began at Simeon. He was the best player on a team made up mostly of upperclassmen. He averaged nearly 20 points per game for the season. He also had eight assists and three **steals** per game.

The coaches at Simeon knew they had a

In his senior year of high school, Derrick (*top row, far right*) anchored the varsity basketball team, shown here.

special player in Derrick. Others saw the same thing. Amateur basketball coach Luther Topps had been watching Derrick since the young point guard was in fifth grade. "He's a freak of nature," said Topps in 2006. "He can shoot. You can be open just for a split second and he'll find you. He just makes people around him better."

Derrick's favorite food is pizza. His favorite actor is Will Smith.

With John Calipari (*right*) as his college coach, Derrick took his game to the next level.

TIGER STAR

By Derrick's senior season in high school, many people thought he was ready for the NBA. It's incredibly rare for a player to go from high school straight to the world's top professional basketball league. Only a few players have ever done it. But in 2005, the NBA made a new rule to prevent such a move. The rule says a player must be out of high school for at least a year before joining the NBA.

Derrick decided to go to college. He chose the University of Memphis. The Memphis Tigers had a history as a strong basketball team. They also had an up-and-coming coach, John Calipari.

Coach Calipari (*far left*) talks to his team during a game in 2007.

Coach Calipari was impressed with Derrick's basketball skills. He was even more excited about how hard the young player was willing to work. "He's a guy who chases greatness," Calipari said. "You have to have the habits and the work ethic to truly chase it. He does."

Derrick (*left*) helped turn the Memphis Tigers into one of the strongest teams in college basketball.

Derrick agreed to hold a **press conference** to announce his decision to go to Memphis. But he had one condition. He wanted to also include two of his teammates from Simeon who were going to other colleges. "They deserve a press conference too," Derrick said.

The Memphis Tigers were already a good team. But with Derrick running the game as the point guard, they became a great team.

Coach Calipari talks to Derrick during a timeout.

The Tigers stormed through most of the competition in 2007–2008. At the end of the season, it was time for the **National Collegiate Athletic Association (NCAA) basketball tournament**. Memphis made it all the way to the championship game before losing to the University of Kansas, 75–68.

Coach Calipari left Memphis after the 2007–2008 season. He became the head basketball coach at the University of Kentucky.

As soon as the championship game was over, people started asking Derrick about his future. Everyone wanted to know if he was going to leave Memphis for the NBA. "I've got to talk to my family about that," Derrick said. "I haven't even been thinking about it yet."

Derrick's family, including his brother Reggie (*left*), helped him make decisions about his future.

GLORY AND PAIN

The Rose family didn't spend much time talking about Derrick's future. Derrick soon announced he was leaving school for the NBA. "I want all of you to know that I loved every minute of my time at the University of Memphis," he said while making the announcement.

It was an especially interesting year for a basketball star from Chicago to enter the NBA **draft**. The Chicago Bulls had the first pick in 2008. It was no surprise that they chose Derrick.

Derrick immediately became a star for his hometown team. He averaged more than six assists and 16 points per game in 2008–2009. He was the obvious choice for the **Rookie** of the Year award. Even better, the Bulls made the

Derrick (*right*) gets ready to pass the ball to a teammate near the net.

Derrick (*right*) is the third Chicago Bulls player in NBA history to receive the Rookie of the Year award.

playoffs. But they lost to the Boston Celtics in the first round.

Chicago made the playoffs both of the next two years. Derrick had helped turn the Bulls into a team that could compete with the best. There were high hopes for the 2011–2012 season.

But then disaster struck. In a game against the Philadelphia 76ers on April 28, 2012, Derrick fell to the floor and gripped his left knee in pain. He had to be helped off the court. Derrick went to the hospital, where he learned he'd injured a **ligament** in his knee.

Derrick struggles to get up after falling and injuring his knee during a game.

The Bulls had won the game. But spirits were low in the locker room. "It's like the saddest win," said Bulls guard Kyle Korver. Derrick would miss the rest of the 2011–2012 season as well as the entire 2012–2013 season.

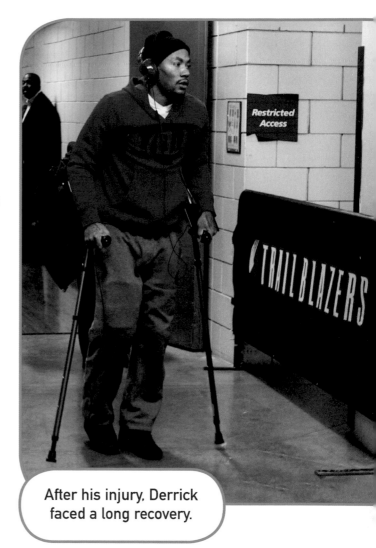

After his injury, Derrick faced a long recovery.

Things were looking up for Derrick and the Bulls at the start of the 2013–2014 season. By November 2013, the team was fighting for a playoff spot. Then Derrick hurt his knee again.

This time, it was his right knee, but the result was the same. He would miss the rest of 2013–2014.

When Derrick was named the NBA MVP in 2011, he became the youngest player to ever win the award.

Knee problems have thrown unexpected obstacles in Derrick's path. But he's determined to bring the NBA championship back to Chicago. He has the talent and drive to do it.

Selected Career Highlights

2013–2014 Averaged 15.9 points and 4.3 assists per game in 10 games for the Chicago Bulls before injuring his right knee

2012–2013 Missed the entire season with a knee injury

2011–2012 Averaged 21.8 points and 7.9 assists per game in 39 games for the Chicago Bulls before injuring his left knee

2010–2011 Named NBA MVP
Averaged 25 points and 7.7 assists per game for the Chicago Bulls

2009–2010 Averaged 20.8 points and 6 assists per game for the Chicago Bulls

2008–2009 Named NBA Rookie of the Year
Averaged 16.8 points and 6.3 assists per game for the Chicago Bulls
Drafted first overall by the Chicago Bulls

2007–2008 Led Memphis to the NCAA championship game
Enrolled at the University of Memphis

2006–2007 Averaged 25.2 points and 8.8 assists per game for Simeon Career Academy

2005–2006 Averaged 20.1 points and 8.7 assists per game for Simeon Career Academy

2004–2005 Averaged 19.8 points and 8.3 assists per game for Simeon Career Academy
Moved up to the varsity team as a sophomore

2003–2004 Won the Chicago city championship with his freshman team

Glossary

assists: passes to teammates that help the teammates score baskets

baseline: the line on the court behind each basket

draft: a yearly event in which professional sports teams take turns choosing new players from a selected group

layups: one-handed shots attempted from close range

ligament: a short, flexible band that connects two bones

National Collegiate Athletic Association (NCAA) basketball tournament: an end-of-the-season competition in which college basketball teams play to decide the national champion

playoffs: a series of games held every year to decide a champion

point guard: a player on a basketball team who is responsible for running the team's offensive plays

press conference: an interview given to a group of reporters to answer questions or make an announcement

rebounds: balls caught after shots to the basket were missed

rookie: a first-year player

slam dunks: when a player slams the basketball through the basket

steals: plays in which defenders take the ball away from the other team

three-point shots: long-range shots that count for three points

varsity: the top sports team representing a school

Further Reading & Websites

Chicago Bulls Website
http://www.nba.com/bulls
The official website of the Bulls includes team schedules, news, profiles of past and present players and coaches, and much more.

Fishman, Jon. *Carmelo Anthony*. Minneapolis: Lerner Publications, 2014.

Kennedy, Mark, and Mike Stewart. *Swish: The Quest for Basketball's Perfect Shot*. Minneapolis: Millbrook Press, 2009.

NBA Website
http://www.nba.com
The NBA's official website provides fans with recent news stories, statistics, biographies of players and coaches, and information about games.

Savage, Jeff. *Dwyane Wade*. Minneapolis: Lerner Publications, 2015.

Sports Illustrated Kids
http://www.sikids.com
The *Sports Illustrated Kids* website covers all sports, including basketball.

LERNER
SOURCE

Expand learning beyond the printed book. Download free, complementary educational resources for this book from our website, www.lernerresource.com.

Index

Photo Acknowledgments

The images in this book are used with the permission of: © Jonathan Daniels/Getty Images, pp. 4, 29; © Scott Strazzante/Chicago Tribune/MCT via Getty Images, p. 5; © Jonathan Daniel/Getty Images, p. 6; © Tannen Maury/Alamy, p. 7; © Kevin C. Cox/Getty Images, p. 8; AP Photo/Charles Cherney, p. 10; Seth Poppel Yearbook Library, p. 10; © Melanie Stetson Freeman/The Christian Science Monitor/Getty Images, pp. 11, 12; John Zich/NewSport/ZUMAPRESS.com/Newscom, pp. 14, 16; Seth Poppel Yearbook Library, pp. 15, 17; AP Photo/Eric Gay, p. 18; AP Photo/David J. Phillip, p. 19; © San Antonio Express-News/ZUMA Press/Icon SMI/Icon SMI, p. 20; AP Photo/Sue Ogrocki, p. 21; Charles Cherney/Chicago Tribune/Newscom, p. 23; Tannen Maury/Newscom, p. 24; KAMIL KRZACZYNSKI/Newscom, p. 25; UPI/Brian Kersey/Newscom, p. 26; Steve Dykes/USA Today Sports/Newscom, p. 27.

Front cover: © Michael Hickey/Getty Images.

Main body text set in Caecilia LT Std 55 Roman 16/28.
Typeface provided by Adobe Systems.